Your Last Day on Earth

Your Last Day on Earth

Carla Hartsfield

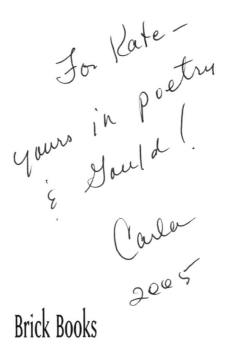

For Kate —
yours in poetry
& Gould!

Carla
2005

Brick Books

National Library of Canada Cataloguing in Publication

Hartsfield, Carla, 1956-
    Your last day on earth / Carla Hartsfield.

Poems.
ISBN 1-894078-31-4

I. Title.

PS8565.A675Y68 2003   C811'.54   C2003-903695-2

We gratefully acknowledge the Canada Council for the Arts, the
Government of Canada through the Book Publishing Industry
Development Program (BPIDP), and the Ontario Arts Council
for their support of our publishing program.

The cover paintings, (left to right "Heat," "Chaos," and
"Hibiscus", watercolour on handmade paper), are by Carla
Hartsfield.

The author's photograph is by Kenneth Ross.

This book is set in Galliard, Mrs. Eaves and Gill Sans.
Design and layout by Alan Siu.
Printed and bound by Sunville Printco Inc.

Brick Books
431 Boler Road, Box 20081
London, Ontario N6K 4G6

brick.books@sympatico.ca

This book is dedicated with loving memory to my father,
Thomas Eugene Hartsfield
(1929-1999)

Contents

III. GOODBYE

I. FLOWERING

I have come to the borders of sleep,
The unfathomable deep
Forest where all must lose
Their way . . .

Edward Thomas, "Lights Out"

Flowering

The night we parted
my drink caught on fire;
news of your betrayal
lit the blackness. Before long,
the whole garden exploded.

My roses were the first to go,
thorns popping and smelling
like a witchhunt.
I stood beneath the fallout,
letting the snaking cinders
sting my arms.

This was catharsis,
to rid myself of jealousy,
your control. Flowering
is never predictable;
these small deaths
have *nothing*
to do with the heart.

Stolen Torch

Look how this Maple in front of my house
drops a brooding leaf every few seconds!
Until there are rings of fallen stars
orbiting the driveway. I count them
methodically as they spindle the dwarf
tree's arthritic hands, each one
transformed and torching
the steps. There's abuse, too,
along the fence behind my son's school—
leaves splattered
against that wire-mesh screen
like photos secreted from a police file;
I say, *I'm sure he did it, no question,*
as a charming pyromaniac
bends every treebranch back.
Fire courses down,
the trees giving up
their masks, their armour.
This is who they're supposed to be.
Prometheus, performance artist,
finally set free.

Towering Hibiscus

I've held your remains.
They were already dry,
misshapen, as though
withered by stroke.
Your DNA cascaded
across my bare feet:
hot confetti, corpuscles,
red stars. Your 24th hour
never wanted to stop.

Were the gods against
you and your stunning twin,
who also imploded minutes later?
It's hard to believe anything
would choose this form,
pen a covenant
with earth's clay soul—
just so ill-wrought plans
could pull heaven
into dust. *What,*

I hear, *it isn't over?*
There are more shows
to come? When I struggle
to erase every disturbing picture,
gold bands perfectly intact
on severed hands
rooting in fire.

Tell me if it will keep
happening this way:
your unscheduled blooms
through the drape of chill air
like a hospital gown—
what's left of you

shrinking into rust-coloured crepe
before grieving is given a chance.

Your last day on earth played
like a looped tape of terrorist footage:
the same body fanned
into brilliant fingers,
the same yellow spotlights
continually lit
then extinguished.

September 11, 2002.

Stranger than Fiction

July and there's fog on the ground.
It drifts over the heads

of heather blooming late,
past the white-and-purple stalks

waving like luscious hair
along the highway.

One would think
it's Brontë country,

except it isn't. Heathcliff, too,
is nowhere in sight.

The car spins forward,
on and on past villages with names

like Goodwood and Tottenham.
So how do we know it's not the moors?

Heathcliff wouldn't scour about
for his lost true love in weather this warm.

During our picnic by a lake so idyllic
it could pass for *trompe l'oeil*—

all I can talk about is that darn fog
misting through the larkspur

like earth angels. *Forest fires*, you say,
huffing your breath out a little.

More fog. I jaunt three paces ahead
knotting into a frazzle.

Why must I see the world
swathed in romance and mystery?

My combustibles involve passion
between two people so hot

their flames would ignite
then extinguish just as quickly,

instead of ashing into low-
smouldering anger.

Everybody knows Heathcliff
and Catherine were the wrong mix

of rose petals, gunpowder
and a thimble of TNT.

Then why do I envy them?
Because their love never melted

into frosty complacency,
cool acid with enough flash

to make heart-stopping smoke.
Later, we hear that forest fires

are indeed hurling black clouds
from Quebec across Ontario,

and for hundreds of miles into Maine
and New England. Stubbornly,

I imagine this angelic form
carrying batches of heather

in the smoke-filled haze,
unspeakably plain—

caught in the snarls
of disappointment and promise,

swelling thicker and thicker
into an erasable screen.

Queen Anne's Lace

It's that time of summer
when winter appears as a ghost,

when fields are capped
with Queen Anne's Lace.

My hands burn to touch them,
are burned if touched—

heat shooting skyward
into amorphous, sylph-like wings.

These starched hexagons quiver
with cocaine bloom, leaving

breath-marks like hieroglyphs
on broken panes. You

winding a bunch into a choker,
get off on dry needles squeezing my neck,

a kind of rustic S & M.
Why not drink the scene down

and me along with it? Chilled
and let loose in a brimming glass

of heirloom blossoms.
White on white on white.

Shining

The trees have always been here.
That's what they want us to think.
How do I know?
I finally heard them today.
I lay down and watched
inexplicable mouths.
Their leafy droning flipped me out.
I saw the pocket mirrors of souls
vibrating in solitary unction.
I thought, *where has my mind been?*
Believing wind infallible
and me, an amateur linguist.
Why listen to these noisy intruders?
To syllables quaking
like random dreams
we hide under quilts,
pretending amnesia.
The prophetic ones.
So much happens to shut up the gifted,
the raw hearts,
human and otherwise,
beating and glistening on a forest floor.
Leave us alone, that's what I tell you.
Forget eternity rushing overhead.
If the trees are lying I'm willing to believe
they didn't really mean it.
I'm trusting in delicacy
and shining.

The Clearing

It began with sun.
And then the lack of it.
And then more sun.
And there were two children,
one just a baby on the shoulders of his dad.
The baby wore a blue jean cap like my father's,
and his chubby legs and sandalled feet
rode clear of brambled trees,
red poison berries,
white-spotted mushrooms;
and the horses, looming, strident animals—
probably seven or eight that clopped and snorted,
barely missed us on our narrow path.
We liked the forest, the hesitant darkness.
We liked the quiet, sort of. But
it was the clearing that got to me:
a shock of wonder transcending
sixteenth-century frescoes,
both wild and ethereal,
landing on our heads.
We wore amazement all afternoon,
hurtling on asteroid wheels
into the sunset, flashing. And at two a.m.
when I passed by the baby's room,
he was still wearing his.
And again this evening.
The funny thing is,
he knows I can see it,
and he keeps putting on his hat
to cover it up. When I check
on him sleeping, my hand
slips under the denim cap-brim,
protective light

from the clearing pouring out
right into my palm.
I push it back in,
this anointing unfamiliar,
too valuable and pure
for the initiate, his mother,
trembling in the nursery.
That's why I let the baby
do what he wants.

Tea Leaves

I knew a psychic who would hold my teacup
on her forehead, marble eyes
staring into a crystalline world.

She saw modern-day highwaymen
ready to steal my songs and poetry.
She saw my father in a hammock

with hatchets flashing like lightning over him,
before a chronic sickness tossed him into the nettles.
She saw my children before they were born,

their twig-like forms
climbing the Statue of Liberty.
She saw Texas wrenched from my side like a rib.

I floated in the fragile curve
of her English china pattern,
an aimless leaf like James Joyce's moon.

※ ※ ※

In the land of seances for doggies and mommies,
I summon a spirit with one simple act.
At Kingsmere overlooking a garden of ruins,

I order the special blend of Canada's
tenth Prime Minister.
Tea-steam conjures the known and unknown,

wafting up my nostrils and out
into the cold, spring day.
Refusing the strainer and steeped

in hot liquid perfect for divination,
I gaze into the reflection
of a face like my face, hair like my hair,

winging gregariously with startled reverence.
Gwendolyn MacEwen
must have met this someone. I'm told

it's Mother King, filtering through porchscreens
or seals on jam jars—
shimmering like air spaghetti

before stirring the tea of unsuspecting guests.
So I drink and pour, drink and pour,
turning my cup bottom up when I'm done.

Those are the rules for reading tea leaves.
You must allow them
to do their work. Stopped in mid-orbit,

my saucer morphs into an undiscovered Pollock,
autumn in chaos
after a freak hailstorm, my mind

after six hours of piano teaching,
long division, lichen mutating—
artifacts clouding any face like my face.

From the tea leaves I rise, fumbling towards
the afterworld—
there's no such thing as only one future.

At the Textile Museum

Like a carpet of autumn leaves, the cloth
rolled out along the dense black wall—

an exuberant pattern of gold
painted on sheer reddish-brown.

I wanted to touch it—and did,
carefully hidden by the gallery wall.

It felt like kissing my grandmother's cheek,
her skin finer and less firm than a baby's—

faint remembrances, since she died
the same year this museum was born.

Today a ceremonial turban pulls me closer,
unfurls like a celebration, saying,

"Undress and lie down—no one will notice."
This immense piece of tie-dyed cloth

plans to claim me—perhaps ink
tiny flames on my white, shivering body.

I suspect the turban could brand a road
through the middle of my head,

burn flowers on my scalp.
Intrigued, I'm patient until

the gallery patrons slip out:
school children with their clipboards,

the curator with his halo
of cotton-spindled hair.

The flame-cloth rises off
a twenty-foot board

until I'm left breathing
inside its sheer cocoon.

Flung into a corner where
only my hair gives me away,

I feel the puncturing of sharp
metal fingernails on muslin,

a tribal beat. This is *my* ceremony,
to clutch cowries and don burial gowns.

The symmetrical patterns finally ignite—
a pyre of rapture and release.

Anonymous

Leaving the elevator and stepping
onto the third floor exhibit,

I'm afraid, startled, as if someone
with a dagger awaits me. My stomach

tightens when the Mali magician's cloak
comes into view. Spiders

instead of leather buttons,
crawl upward in marathon columns,

the disengaged remnants of ruined webs
dangling from the bottom of its weedy hem.

Rounding the frightful corner
to meet my assassin, invisible bodies

shove me instead, rushing toward
my face and neck. I try

to catch my breath as the outline
of a glowing form whizzes past.

The light is liquid gold,
dazzling and quivering

into a pot-bellied Burden Basket.
Trembling auras leak

from willow and dogwood.
The masks are laughing at me,

laugh at each other.
Their straw beards and pointed hats

making me feel six again,
the outcast at my sister's

birthday party. Is this the reason
I long to be anonymous?

Let me tell you a story. It's about
riding the subway on a freezing

grey Wednesday, mid-winter,
when the trees rose like barren

stalks out of the ground—
their hairy bark, matted and itchy

as the Japanese rain cape a few feet away.
Hours pass before I realize what I've done,

before the loss of my purse
drops over my arm like a shadow.

It was a small black knapsack,
multi-pocketed and zippered,

washable micro-fiber—nothing as valuable
as purses woven in the mountains of Timor,

those lasting a lifetime and hung
on poles to signal one's death.

But without my purse I *feel* dead.
Without my S.I.N. number I don't exist.

Without makeup my eyes disappear
like threads in a carpet. Then this

unearthly voice finds a channel.
It tells me to be euphoric.

The voice claims I'm free to wander
the world as a nameless soul.

I'm no longer tied to my credit cards.
During the next twenty-four hours

only my husband minds that he's
married to Ms. Anonymous,

a breathing, whirling copy of me.
When the purse resurfaces

at Lost & Found, the world cries
How lucky! to be spared that burden

of redemption. Every photo,
penny, receipt in its place.

A miracle! I laugh.
Like a criminal escaping

I'd almost done it
without showing my birthmark—

a lace-like etching
on my upper left thigh.

Here is my postscript: there are others like me
in the Textile Museum. They try on

the rain cape, hide in baskets,
sell their tapestry purses

to unknowing teenagers.
They come back to claim them

when the moon is full
and the gardens are hardening

with frost. *Stand still and listen,*
hold out your hand,

open and close your eyes
while these beings pulse,

amorphous and god-like
among the living, pressing

their shapeless, unpronounceable
heat into yours.

Black-Eyed Susans

Me after the party. Them
after the hottest summer on record—way North.
Me pulling an all-nighter in university. *Twice*. Them
when the water's rationed,
when the dog pees on the bush,
when the well-meaning gardener forgets to clear weeds,
thinking *surely these aren't weeds*. Me
at twelve trying on makeup for the first time.
My dress is psychedelic
and breasts non-existent,
dark buds beginning to hum. Them
surrounded by gaudy mums,
by dahlias and their toe-roots,
by asters turning smeared faces toward heaven—
confused, aggressive, exhilarated. Me
after the boyfriend break-up,
mascara charcoaled onto tee-shirts and sleeves. Them
huddled with frightened glances in pool-table yards,
blown by the heat of barbecues and families,
before frost exhumes their pungent light. Me
in another life named Sue
or Susie or Susannah,
picking bee-coloured suns,
strolling in a field of Them.

Flame Roses

December and heat rises from a dozing plant—
middle of the garden, no leaves,

no prickly touching, no light
except for these two petalled flames

smouldering with pleasure. *And yet.*
Cloudless days keep spilling

into back alleys and garbage cans,
pouring dry ice onto the flame roses,

electric and vain. This tiny bush
prays with attitude. I pay rent

while the flame roses melt phobias
and Seasonal Affective Disorder.

The center of my chest cavity
is where their mania resides.

They ponder El Niño, my
strung-out wiring—and each other.

The comforter sizzles. Burn patches appear
like stigmata on my ribs.

Daisies

Faces struck with the brightness
of subnormal winds; the daisies
quiver, sort of damaged.
They open with little cracks,
their whiteness stretched,
their tart bindings
stunned by glass.
Why are the daisies astonished?
And why this severing tension?
I could make surreal daisies anytime.
By stepping into freezing-sharp puddles.
By kissing cold windows.
By pulling on eighty-eight keys
lined up like dozens of petals—
their stinging beauty disrupting
the blackest fissures.
And the ache that arrives
as I move my hands
through passage after passage;
this music is spiked and dangerous,
altering the continent of my piano lid.
Daisies are crowned with fatal intuition.
They meet me head on
with a vibrant and lethal
scent of refusal.

Empty Beds

I'm speaking from below,
as a bulb tucked away for the winter,
as wilted iris plowed under.

I was always exhausted as a child.
I blame piano lessons—
those repetitive scales,
somnolent hymns barely endured.
After practicing, still clothed,
I'd faint crossways on a chair,
rushed into delirious silence.

Nothing could wake me,
not my mother's persistent shaking,
not the light switch flipped on and off.
I was dead to the world
for a good ten hours—
and then it ceased.
Adolescent narcolepsy.

I learned to drink coffee
and get my second wind.
I learned to grow
an invisible sheath.

This is what I knew:
people were listening to secrets
pulsing inside my head.
That foreign, untapped drama.
Origins of an authentic self
trying to form.

How I wanted to please.
How I've *wanted*, just wanted.

Like I said, I'm speaking
from a legacy of empty beds.
After years of sleep trauma,
I must go back
into the tangled sheets
of archetypal wanderings,
down to that twelve-inch space
draped with *faux* bedskirts,
where nosy, degenerate figures
lie in wait. Maybe

if I get really dirty,
cover myself completely,
sleep for centuries
and quit asking who I once was,
I won't need conversations
with limpid branches
or angelroot stems.
I'll shed life after life
dropping onionskin casings
on a coldroom floor—
it won't matter where I rest,
or that I'm just too tired to undress.

The Dark

Come in here.
It's soothing, worthwhile.
Let's slide through *Abstraction 28*
and lick the surface.
The colour is almost more
than I can stand,
deep burgundy—
not lost in black velvet
like some Elvis painting.

I'm more elated by O'Keeffe's
purpling dark
than a lapsed teetotaller filling
a tub full of sherry.
This is a place Dickinson wouldn't go,
even if her eyes
did match the bathtub ring.

Here, we can be naked.
Here, we can position ourselves
in front of Georgia's
textured canvas
and surrender in delight.

The dark becomes us,
opening gradually
onto a drunken sea.
I see myself drawn,
line by line.
And you crying out
as your tongue dips in.

Nightshine

She was here inside the purple-eyed daisies
and honeysuckle lining the fence—

arriving seconds after visiting the moon,
her starched, white dress

cascading from frothy clouds—
but even more white like the light

that is said to emanate from reverence;
everything she touches extols circumference,

cool gowns and day lilies, wings
that have never taken flight but need to,

unsure feet touching windy stretches of sand—
she believes that she's guiding us through

the fragile terrain of complex thought,
like flowers lit from within

beneath a sky so transient, visions
must be stolen from Nightshine

and magnified against infinity;
she is here to tell us that real illumination

lives in the space between
wrong rhyme and wronged hearts—

how those spaces glowed with phobic energy,
her diminutive form captured in lace;

in the twenty-first century,
if we are privy to the genius

of flowers in humble yards
or stumble across unexplained light

lingering over the rosemary and lavender—
we should pay more attention

to these earthbound heavens;
someone, maybe Emily,

is showing us how to transcend,
bloom beyond recognition.

In the Garden

Here are my first trilliums!
Perky little starched cuffs,
pristine as a Tour Ontario ad,
ready to propel out
of their garden-green skins.
Me too. That's why
I'm in the garden.

I've been like Psyche lately
tramping through hell,
paying the price for not trusting in fate.
I've fled to Providence, literally,
a retreat center protected by
the Audubon Society
and unseen garden wizards.

Spent the afternoon
crouched in the belly
of an ancient tree.
Climbed up there on a ladder
and bent myself into the shape
of an acorn to meditate.
That's when the Mallard
paddled by, feathers
iridescent as abalone.
He was trying to swim upstream.
I thought I was hallucinating.
Hey, you're no salmon I yelled,
except I was working on
achieving a state of serenity;
I zipped my karmic self shut.

That's when the Mallard took off.
Just flew out of there at an angle so sharp,

the water reeds were ducking.
It made sense. Why stick around
when you can't follow your chosen path?

Mine began in a country
that wasn't handed to me at birth.
I've tried twice to grow bluebonnets,
the Texas state flower,
but the seeds froze on the ground
and wouldn't leaf in my neighbour's
greenhouse. One could say,
they were out of their habitat.

I will never get used to ice pellets
raining from the sky in May.
Or the crystal-cut impartiality
of stars misaligned in a northern sky.

Yes, I've been brooding
in the garden. While the trilliums
stare open-mouthed,
daring me to steal them.
Better to wander with Psyche
through Rodin's gates for a few more days.
She and I have unfinished business.
It's called Providence. It's called
finishing the journey.

II. MUSES

"We could pretend to be gods if we knew how a God acted…"

Paulette Jiles, "Life in the Wilderness"

Angel of Emergency

Fasting, driving to the lab
oncoming headlights puncture my vision
as if the needle can't possibly miss.

I drink a bottle of glucose
that smears my blood
into fantastic orange puddles,
breeds sugar hallucinations,
cells of fear.

A white-coated figure
stands over me, waiting.
The word *breathe* floats down,
but the vial is empty—
my tiny veins rolling,
familiar hurts. Earlier

I'd listened in the car
to the Death March Sonata:
pages of needle scratchings
banging in sync
to the frenzied doors
of a nearby phonebooth.

Then a lilting voice says *got it*—
great pockets of wind
sting the hospital parking lot,
relief flies over me
on Plexiglas wings.

Every phonebooth in the city
becomes my angel of emergency,
pumps blood from my arm
to Chopin's finale.

When Angels Dance in that Tiny Blackness

The heart is musical,
its semi-lunar flaps

of membrane singing
as blood pulses through.

Sometimes my heart
skips a beat,

the mitral valve prolapsed,
especially cranky

at high altitudes. My younger son
was born with a hissing leak

that closed after six months.
I saw it first in the cardiologist's office,

disbelieving—the pin-sized hole
bobbing up in the middle

of a fancy scanner. There were
angels dancing in that tiny blackness,

and then they were gone.
Why am I thinking about this now,

after healing? Because
the four chambers of the heart

are profound. They speak from
air, fire, earth and water.

One chamber cannot do
without another chamber,

and even when flow is cut off
the heart tissue beats freely.

This image plays in my mind,
hot and cold colours

moving in waves around tough,
air-pressured walls.

This same heart looks like Flight 587
leaving Kennedy airport, flying

between the fifth and sixth ribs of sky.
On the cardiologist's monitor

you see what the air traffic controller sees,
a plane zooming from the screen,

splitting into four parts. We focus
on Rockaway where 587 crashed,

the air charred with shock,
blood-letting, blood-letting.

Because the plane is musical,
it thumps and sings I ♥ N Y,

the Twin Tower disaster
still smoldering.

The wreckage of Flight 587
summons the four elements

like new patron saints.
And I again see my son's heart

swerving and dipping
in a specialist's office,

each chamber on fire
touching down

soaked with tears. When angels
dance in that tiny blackness

they want the same thing
that everyone wants:

to keep the heart singing,
no matter what.

Camouflaged

A robin sits on a grey-limbed branch
eyeing me straight in the face.
He doesn't budge

and neither do I.
It's April and this robin
is already plump.

He's eaten well
through the mild winter,
and is hunting for more.

Maybe he's stolen from other birds,
camouflaged as a blue jay
or sharp-beaked raven to feast.

Ah, thievery. How much loss can we stand?
When my best pair of gloves were stolen,
a fashionable camouflage print—

I saw red. Me, who hates to wear gloves
in any season. When you look at my hands
do you see violence, hatred?

Do you see words or music
fluttering from my fingertips—
massages given, babies diapered?

Do you see blood drenching
an old kitchen towel,
after the knife-edged corner

of a Roland keyboard
sliced my tendon? The scar
on my left hand third finger

is shaped like a frown
and prays to disappear daily. Why cover
my hands with combat material?

Am I ashamed? Am I?
The night my gloves
were stolen at Holy Joe's

I drove home, then back
hoping to ferret out the stealer,
make somebody feel sorry.

But, they were all like Robin Red Breast,
staring ahead, self-satisfied,
different from the first flock.

This crowd was certain
my gloves and I *didn't*
invade their territory.

Camouflaged. And they hid
so pleasantly behind their faces,
pleased to have stripped

my hands and hope bare,
what feeds and warms
and forgives.

Meeting Leon Fleischer at the Corner of Bedford & Bloor

I tend to think it was unavoidable—
playing K. 570 for him
at the University of Texas.

Or fated as one of Fleischer's surgeries,
scars notated onto his right hand,
spelling out *unlucky*.

A spirit above skates the twilight moon—
it's Schubert with a pockmarked face
like a driving range.

For the second time in my life
I'm poised at a precipice with Leon Fleischer,
light singing the *Wandererfantasie*.

We're both coming back
to the conservatory from dinner,
and he looks formidable

with his tousled hair and woollen scarf.
I'm rigid with awe, uttering
thank you's to Ravel and Scriabin,

Leon's swarthiness marching closer.
Without the D major Concerto
and left-hand études

Fleischer would be conducting
on the dark side—
propping that silent hand

on his old LPs, each note
greying in some vinyl crater.
How many musicians

including myself,
have been lured into nine feet
of glistening, black chasm?

Where the only music playing
is blood trying to course
through nerve damaged fingers.

Instead *we chat*, Leon and I.
He thinks he remembers my clean
but homegrown version of Mozart.

"Your face is not unfamiliar,"
he booms politely. Schubert
the wingless apparition,

stands briefly between his shoulders,
a chorus of nightsky flooding
Varsity stadium. Even before

he unwinds that surgery-ridden hand
to say goodbye, I'm sure
I've never seen anything like it.

With mine locked into his
we fly to our studios without aid
of limbs or instruments;

no need to wait for the go-ahead signal
at the corner of Bedford & Bloor;
there are other ways to continue.

Ripped Off

I'm in a hotel listening to Schubert.
It's the E minor Sonata,
not one of his best—
maybe because he ripped off Beethoven
and felt guilty. Why am I here?

Oh, yeah—marking exams.
Meanwhile, the curtain's open
and vintage blocks of glass
heat up the room, my face
flushed. The first movement

cadences crudely,
and a guy by the pool
takes off his shirt, his image
doing the Andy Warhol thing
inside my make-shift kaleidoscope.

After the Allegretto
he taps out a cigarette.
Now I'm upset.
It's too soon to light up.
I'm supposed to be listening,

but this James Dean look-alike
is showing off a set of bulging pecs.
Fortunately, someone else
is marking with me, and she's
so engrossed in the music

I'm relying on her disinterest
in virtual sex
to keep her eyes flowing
down the legal-size marking slip.
My guy takes a dive

as the third movement begins,
his body curving into a muscular phrase,
the lean sinew of his arms and legs
kicking through cross-currents
of wronged notes,

waves belonging to frozen margaritas
and Antiquity. What's left of my brain
after that shirt came off
sent me swimming back
to circa 1827. I'm the lady

swooning when the teenaged Liszt
swaggered into Schubert's soiree.
Liszt never smoked
and had the decency to check in
to a monastery at forty.

Wearing a silken robe
and rock star hair,
he communed with angels
as a celibate composer.
I guess it's all in the fantasy—

how art never imitates art.
Except at the moment.
I've been celibate
for two weeks and have hated
every second of it.

That's a lie. As all
performances are. Poets
imagine they've fallen in love.
Musicians strum the hard-luck ballad.
It's time to close the curtain.

"And the hours of practicing, my ear
Tone deaf and yes, unteachable,
I learned, I learned, I learned elsewhere,
From muses unhired by you, dear mother."
"The Disquieting Muses"
Sylvia Plath

The Princess of Balakirew*

is petite and dark, eyes
black with secrets;

she's the sort of girl
Sylvia should have listened to—

she doesn't know the meaning
of wooden scales or stiff arabesques.

Like a rare, poised bird,
the princess is a cadenza in flight,

her jet-blue ponytail dipping
like a butterfly minus the madam.

She's the sort of girl
Ted Hughes would have flown to—

mysterious intellectual performing "The Lark."
She can lure you with her sound,

sweet and sustained and fluffy as whipped cream
before it melts on your tongue.

The Princess of Balakirew
plays the piano with bloodied wings,

shining from practice.
She's the sort of girl

clever enough to save anyone
with her music—especially Sylvia

sulking in shadow. The energy soars
from Balakirew's heart, huge

as a Viking's. She doesn't know Plath
once etched word images

like pen-and-ink drawings,
while crows plotted to kill her,

arching in lyric rows
on the score of her mind.

When the princess unleashes her ponytail
for the final run, great sighs breathe out

from both girls—their vocal cords
vibrating like unstrung piano wire.

Here are the muses freed of competition,
comforting themselves and the world.

Balakirew transcribed Gluck's vocal song "The Lark" for solo piano

Brahms & Angelo's Garage

It might be the perfect way to listen to a concerto.
The parking lot of an east-end McDonald's.
CBC radio and the New York Philharmonic.
A Sausage McMuffin, hold the egg.
New Technology plugged
into The Age of Enlightenment.
1962 and Lenny Bernstein.
Glenn Gould conducting his
special-order intellect from a corner in Fran's,
where he ate a plate of eggs
every morning over the papers.
And managed headlines in the key of D minor
with his week-long rehearsal
of a quirky standard.
Then there's me and Angelo
next to an American standard—
stick shift, that is. He's
using his wrench like a maestro—
car parts vibrate; at least
I hear low-level humming going on.
But maybe that's Gould making counterpoint
where only he can hear it—
though *it's right, it's incredible;*
whenever I play Brahms I need larger arms,
kind of like Angelo here. I need a brawny body,
a five o'clock shadow, and unmuffled tone
motoring to the back row of Carnegie Hall.
I'm halfway through my Sausage McMuffin,
and Gould is making his way through
the second harmonic transition
in the extended, contrapuntal recapitulation;
I see the whole orchestra as a toolbox
with bolts (wind section),
nuts (strings, *especially violas*),
drills (trumpets and horns),

tubes hanging down from hydraulic lifts
(percussion and harp). Nobody thought
Brahms should sound like this,
except Gould and Brahms and me
trying hard not to get monkey grease
or cheese grease onto any part of our
not-yet-dead musical anatomies.
Nobody expected, especially Bernstein,
that *he* might be wrong—
Gould in his youth
had the idea of the century.
To project Brahms like fine, curved chrome.
To shine it up into a vintage car.
To get the dumbbell piston
to meet the pianist halfway.
When the fine-tuning is done
what you're left with is Glenn—
brilliant and shy in a leatherette booth
enjoying his breakfast, the sheen
still crystal on his genius.
And *the eggs, the eggs,*
because a Toronto cook
cranked them out so fast.
Are you listening, Lenny,
now that the mechanics and critics
have assembled into one
symphonic entity in Angelo's garage?
Hear Gould emanating boldly
with original lightness
into the recycled cup
that got stuck in the pipe.

Playing Mr. J.S. Naked

Fresh from the shower,
towel draped Roman-style,
you choose freefall into the Sarabande,
an 18th c. dance.
Drops of ornamentation
splatter diamonds on your skin,
and leave signature grace notes
drying on your piano's veneer,
its curvy black.

Secretly, you've performed this way before.

Who can glimpse how the towel
slides past your slim, weak ankles
and pedalling toes—
how that move coincides
with Bach-ian sliders,
thirty-seconds twisting
into figure eights,
the fractal version
of Cosmology for Dummies.

Mr. J.S. is making you use
both sides of your brain
and all of your body. *How dare he.*
Fugues are like stepping into
a hall of mirrors.
And his strettos
have nothing to do with librettos
or ghetto Hip Hop
or hating piano practice and SpaghettiOs
when you were a kid.
Strettos are slow, real slow—
the music streaming inward
like transcendental meditation

Yeah, here you are
playing the Baroque version
of Oscar Peterson,
your fingers tripping out
with eighty-eight slicks in tuxedos—
and while you're strutting the Sarabande
skin to wood
bone to metal
mouth to ivory resuscitation,
you've never felt so exposed
or ecstatically good
in your unclad awakening.
Just say dance, girl.
Dance for one.

Three's a Charm

My neighbour has chopped down
the mulberry bush without asking.
Leapt across my herb garden
fragrant in late bloom,
hacking at it like a man
licensed to kill. I stand
at my kitchen window
and allow this to happen,
marvelling at his urgency,
as if the mulberry is burning,
ready to spout prophecies.

Who invented the lines
three's a charm or
bad things come in threes?
Why should three
possess so much power,
when it's only the root
of that mystical, infinite nine.

I'm weary of this war.
Not of the mulberry
thrice springing up
bearing blood-black fruit;
but of my neighbour's conviction
that the bush should be growing
on his side—he claims
to have planted the original
sometime. And nothing of his,
not the fennel or tomatoes
or three types of basil
may seed on enemy soil.
Yet they do.

He's finished stacking
and binding the branches,

face splashed with sour liqueur.
The words *how dare you*
throb in my temples.
It's the colour, you see,
of the berries—
or if you'd prefer,
the mingled blood
of Pyramus and Thisbe.

The plan to elope
was their first mistake.
To meet at the white mulberry
by the Tomb of Ninus
was their second.
Soon, these secret lovers
would willingly fall
on a death-pact sword
one   two   three; the mulberry
had no choice
but to dye its fruit
the colour of mourning.

When I confront my neighbour
he turns more black
than the stench of robbery
uneaten and smashed
on his fingers. Like most criminals
he pleads not guilty—then
no longer speaks to me,
a curious way to break
our little feud. When
the mulberry grows back
I'm expecting fruit
so sugary and white,
even the gods
won't go near it.

Bound to Silence

Wanting keepsakes
for my solitary room,
something that says
this is yours, truly,
I search for quartz
finding two lone pinks
among the grey-flannel stones.
Bare of artifice, the crystals
steal deftly into my pocket,
bound to their world
of silence.

At the retreat center
I am also bound.
I must not play my harp.
I take reverent walks
over the craggy
evolution of lakes,
and munch carrot cake
next to nameless visitors.

Is this the opposite of chaos?
Non-linear physics claims
that theory doesn't exist.
Weather patterns skip
to their own beat,
and avalanches start easier
than my harp snapping a string.

In 1970 I saw a jaggedy rock
flying like a meteor
out of my cousin's hand;
it landed with full impact
on my sister's mouth.

After her tooth was capped
the dentist found seventeen cavities.

See what I mean? My sister
couldn't speak for weeks.
And here I am
with metaphysical cotton
stuffed in my mouth.

Roman myths warned
of this silent chaos,
a mist-like body from which
all things are born;
I'm encased inside
holding hands with Muta,
a tape of my life
paused.

Miss _____

She wears a sky-blue smock dress, more pale than her china-doll eyes. When she climbs onto the piano bench, rivulets of tawny hair swing in tandem with her white leather shoes. Her porcelain legs are still-lifes, too short to touch the floor. She sits onstage looking as if she could scatter secrets like rose petals down the aisle at a wedding. Her innocent bourrée bounces with such clarity, the stained-glass windows in the sanctuary sigh. No other experience has prepared me for a mute child. For this psychic force-field, abrasive silence. *Miss _____ doesn't speak to adults,* the note said, information so cryptic, its author might be ashamed. At some point this girl will need to speak to me. So Miss _____ brings flash cards drawn with black marker. Facing away, she whips them out aggressively, poised on her right shoulder like rectangular birds. She must be left handed, *mano sinistra*. In olden days a non-speaking child would be pegged sorceress, friend of Satan, her left hand up to no good. Is the aura surrounding her on fire? Does she talk to familiars? Hear transmuted dialects for the godly or wicked? Her playing is flawless; I begin to think of her like my Chatty Cathy doll, who stopped talking after we both flew into an out-of-control steering wheel. A fissure opened at the base of her neck, the pull-chain never snapping back. Weeks after the car accident I held Cathy hopefully, yanked on her voice-string, pressed my fingers into the cut threatening her speech *right there*—praying for a mere syllable. The doll's blushing lids would open shut, shut open, producing sound like the soft click of a key before the hammer makes contact. *Vibrations.* In *The Piano,* Holly Hunter's character stopped talking because she found her ultimate mouthpiece. The same could be true of Miss _____. Or did an adult, perhaps her father, deliver warnings at bedtime? *No one must know the cause of her fears.* When I forget myself and bend too close, the child turns on her heel, stares me down, runs toward the parking lot shrouded in graceful, haunted terror.

Black Lace & Trees

In the space between their branches
and my heart, I feel the webbing.

It pulls me closer to the August deaths
in this graveyard—except it's October, isn't it?

While my young sons catch pirouetting leaves,
I see evidence of crewelwork, as tiny sticks

lock fingers, joints and nails. Once
women would make reams of black lace

until their vision swam with rosettes
like shells dotting a shoreline.

Mortality was the star and black lace
its precious advertiser. And when

I see my sons giggling and rolling
in these webs of cold fire,

I find it difficult to look, rather,
turn and hear a chorus, *three chords only*—

as clouds release the antidote
to black lace, clear light

vibrating in four-part harmony.
This is what the soul wants every hour.

Do you believe me? My husband is uncertain.
And I haven't mentioned it to my children;

you might hear these high-pitched chords
as you wade into an ocean, seaweed

churning over water-smoothed stones.
This singing is so alluring

you don't want to swim out of danger.
You might continue to be swept along

as if you're Vivaldi lacking an end
to *The Four Seasons.* When we leave

I notice how treebark is scored
with rough, ill-timed melodies.

How effortless their black lace,
the grooves like hair jewellery.

Did I hear the late cadence of those
mournful deaths coming up for air?

Song endings, impossible,
to brush away.

III. GOODBYE

"But in the grave, all, all, shall be renewed."

W.B. Yeats, "Broken Dreams"

"I don't know why you say goodbye, I say hello."

Lennon & McCartney

The Unbearable Lightness of Being

Did you see the movie? I never did.
My hearing so sensitive
that sound plus visuals plus height

plus movement, equal an assault.
After my father died sensory perception
reached a crisis point. Sometimes

I listened to Rachmaninoff's Third,
his favourite concerto,
and wished for tornadoes

setting electrical currents off in my numb,
getting more numb body. My father,
the physicist—who claimed

he couldn't remember dreams.
I wondered if he'd heard of Freud or Jung
or anyone who thinks dreams are important.

I didn't believe him, because I pictured his psyche
whirring round and round in this petalled windmill
next to his red barn. And though I never saw

The Unbearable Lightness of Being,
I remember that couple blurring the screen
in a five-minute trailer of light and exuberance—

as if any cyclone, emotional or otherwise,
could spin me into the turbulence
of my father's spirit.

These days, what sweeps me off my feet?
J.M. Heade's magnolias, intangibly back-lit,
tag sale paintings fetching a million at auction,

The photographs of Man Ray, more white petals,
and Patty Griffin singing "Flaming Red, Flaming Red."
I hit the treadmill to find my unbearable lightness of being,

until the breathlessness and endorphins take over.
Until I forget about my father's denial
of REM sleep. And Rachmaninoff

tearing through the forbidden darkness.
Now it's my father's windmill,
feather-light and yielding.

Over and over, his dream petals turn.

Plain Geometry

My son is fascinated by circles.
When he was two weeks old
his hands conducted symphonies
from the stroller—air-strokes
going round and round.

What music drove those dimpled fingers,
what colours? Then the kiddy toys
began evolving: electronic cars
with horns, metal or wooden trains.

Descending into the playroom,
the devastation was clear—
trucks overturned,
a multi-vehicle pileup.

Lovingly he would go to each
and keep their wheels spinning
like a magician juggling plates.

Even his body won't stop twirling.
On rugs in front of mirrors,
he somersaults, toes pointed,
giggling and dancing.

Because my father was a whiz at math,
my head revolves with the irony.
Could I, victim of my right brain,
have given birth to the next
Stephen Hawking, or God forbid,
Bill Gates? In restaurants

John makes circles with his milk.
When the waitress brings his glass,
he's elated to see the right amount
of frothy stuff slopped out the sides.

And there he goes
painting one after another
until they criss-cross or stack
like ancient symbols,
miniature crop circles. Clock time,

with its dreaded ticking
toward old age and death
will be of no interest. He's too busy
inventing new laws with my pie plate
and biscuit cutter, hatbox
and spindles of ribbon.

As I excavate bowls
and rolling pins from the yard,
my son chases proofs
on his circular path,
uncorking a hurricane of stars.

Commas

I obsess over them.
Especially now, correcting,
poring over a new collection
soon in print; I first
wipe them out, then
put them back in,
making Madame Bovary
and her mad excesses
look like Mother Theresa.

Without punctuation
showing us how to breathe,
to organize and dramatize,
would anyone know how
our work should sound?
Oh, probably.

I imagine language going the way
of the spotted owl,
the African violet I forgot to water,
half of all marriages,
a computer on its third birthday,
and the study of Latin—
if not already obsolete
in their various stages,
one can expect that dissolution,
strange antimatter of the cosmos
to start humming a dreaded
one-syllable word.

Death.

I take comfort in finding out
I'm not the only maimed soul
passionate about phrasing,

microscopic pauses. Jane Kenyon
amended her final book,
Otherwise, "in the first
five days of her dying,"
writes Donald Hall,
adding a single comma
to "Insomnia at the Solstice."
And that lone comma
was found in her reading copy
after death. Do commas

only matter to poets?
I search the poem,
try to determine where
and why adding a comma
on one's deathbed
should make a difference.
Her poem is musical
with personal resonance,
humorous. Yet, one glorious place
seems suspect, the line
no blanket, or even a sheet.
Austere and symbolic,
mysteriously separated,
that small break would matter
to a dying person, relinquishing
the ethereal body, the breath.
I stop beating up on perfectionism.

In my forty-seventh year, the age
Kenyon passed into spirit,
I adjust my manuscript,
grateful that I don't have to
swallow poison or become a saint
to prove why my voice exists in the world.

New Moon

Why are some miracles more obvious than others?
Talk to me of that web of red clouds
falling from my womb. Tell how
you found me at my kitchen sink,
watching a universe
of fruit and vegetables
spiralling. Beyond
I see the beginning of form,
call it preternatural,
fringed by the curiosity
of worrisome stars. *Never mind.*
I'm not given to revealing secrets—
besides, we've been friends
for an eternity. Maybe you're
my only. Most days
I trust the rhythm of your orbit,
your thumbnail grin,
your full-faced spying
as I cradle the baby. Tonight
you've given me something new:
this lovely, barren circle.
A place to speak and stand
where no one can hurt me:
mysterious well refusing to echo
until your ancient lid
bends open with light.
And that's the worst, isn't it,
when unwanted faces and voices
appear? You didn't know
that the less visible miracle
is the thing I most want—
my own tenebrous circle.

In the Space that My Father Left

after his death, the women
in my family are gathering.
They know what to do,
how to clean up after,
where the dust motes of skin cells
carrying his essence, hide.
They smile demurely
performing this work,
sweeping cobwebs in doorframes
until white and gleaming; while
uncles and nephews left behind,
stare at limestone broken open,
wait to lower the shiny, grey casket,
before taking boutonnieres
fluted and swollen like eyelids—
throwing them down and down.

But the women keep washing dishes
and warming food. They circle
the tables wearing gingham aprons,
their faces placid and oracular
as Madonnas. When they speak
it's to say, "More iced tea?"
or "Have a piece of pie"—
knowing that the apple strudel
and fried chicken we swallow
could not be eaten by him
in the end. So we catch up
on family lore to invoke
my father's presence—
the men sullen and the women
clasping hands to ward off
everybody's fear.

I refuse to wear black on funeral day,
though for Family Visitation
black-and-grey trees swath my arms,
immortal souls, webby and veined,
wander like a highway map
across my chest. When I bought
this blouse, I didn't know
I would wear it standing
over my father's coffin
in Boze-Mitchell Funeral Home—
staring at a permanent grimace
I've never seen before. And
with his body just inches away,
the space he has left
grows unfathomable.
I'm washed away home
to my parents' farm
where the urge to clean,
to pick up a broom
and sweep the patio,
almost overtakes me.
I write a eulogy instead,
preserving not erasing,
charting the years,
unwithered and breathing
through his pecan trees.

The women polish furniture
and run their Hoovers.
They load the dishwashers
and bag the garbage.
This is how they mop up sorrow,
with spongy J-cloths tossed
into Hefty bags. And the men

not participating in this ritual,
cart away chicken bones
and memories, the greasy
napkins and chosen epithets.
The men are shy about
circling and clasping hands.
Because they stand
in purgatory between
mourning and acceptance.
Because they expect the women
to make coffee and serve cake.
Because they must respond
when the widow says,
"Close the lid now,"
and "Please, could you hold
my hand all the way there?"

The night before my father died
I couldn't sleep. He was already
travelling into the afterworld,
pulling me along with him. And
in the farmhouse where he once
set up his model trains,
a boyhood labyrinth of dreams,
his now-gaunt form nudges me
through glistening doorframes
toward the bathroom.
The electric shaver,
recharging there,
belongs to him.
Black as a hearse,

rotary dials encased in plastic,
green on-light blinking—
the shaver keeps my father,
strangely, sort of alive.
In my mind, the women
appear like Furies,
cleaning rags in hand.
They scrub everything—
the sink, the tiles, the mirror.

Here is a space my father still occupies,
evidence of their sloppy handiwork,
proof that the men have some control.
To save electricity, I reach up
to unplug the shaver,
and then, think better of it.

What She Sees

Fresh-painted plaster
dripping like clotted cream
into the baby's crib;
the unshaven face
of her black-hearted husband
kissing the wrong woman.

Then the ice trees drop
frightening mirrors at her feet.

She watches herself break
beyond recognition—
a choir of Sylvias wanting more,
fame exploding
into literary ether.

Here's a thermometer measuring
her fevered writing;
a typewriter ribbon
like a missing lock of hair;
her voice round and round
on a BBC recording.

And the cause of her anger speaks from Pan
in a maze of bee bonnets possessed by Hughes.

He steals her psyche
burned with jealousy,
and she sees him stuffing it
into the trunk of their car,
the one that won't start.

Now Plath stands outside herself.
This can't be her reaching
for scissors and tape.
Or sealing her children
with cookies and milk
behind the doorjamb.

This wandering self peers in
with confused pleasure
to a corner of the gas oven,
witnesses the cradling of her
schoolmarm-ish braid.

But, where is her fragile soul?
Can she still see it gripping
mordant love,
and the insulated shell
of dawn arriving?

Smith College, Graduation Day

Black hats dip and swoop like paper cut-out birds.
Who thinks of suicide while tassels and gowns

darkly flirt down ribboned pathways? Beyond
the hangman bridge stretched like bloody tracks

over Ted's face. Today Plath's future rivals
shrouded in party gear, march to Elgar—

believing that suffused clouds stirring above them
have nothing to do with her jealous presence—

that diplomas embossed with old lettering and seals
will keep them from marrying their fathers' doubles.

Sylvia might be amused at applause erupting
in unrhymed verse, at the unenlightened mob

on the common like crows after the kill—
that they all bothered showing and dressed so well.

Marilyn Monroe on St. Clair Ave.

Spring and clouds furrow brows
like jealous twins. A woman struggles

with a baby carriage, the old-fashioned kind,
bump grind, bump grind—lifting it over

curbs and sewer grates, her too-soft belly
like a deflated balloon after the pregnancy.

She doesn't want to look at her figure displayed
in window-glass like a cute, bovine ceramic.

She doesn't want to cut calories or add
fat-free foods to her already bland diet.

She doesn't want to think about her husband
dreaming of women who torture derrières

into size-four skirts or who sport legs
hard enough to break a bottle on.

She thinks of Ella Fitzgerald and how
she shattered glass for Memorex,

and misses her terribly—Ella's
silky voice seducing the masses.

No liposuction or implants there.
A woman with suspiciously taut thighs

legs it past wearing a pair of cut-off shorts
the size of her baby's diaper and covering less.

The baby sleeps as clouds knit into frowns so huge
they compete with her postpartum depression.

If Van Gogh were here she'd ask him to take
a hunk of her flesh instead of his ear.

Hot wind pants from unlocked doors
and subway tunnels, from accountants' briefcases

and the cleavage of secretaries jiggling in lace teddies,
from her circle skirt fanning into a Tilt-a-Whirl ride

out of control. She flings herself against a building
as workmen stare at her ill-chosen underwear

and untanned legs. There is nowhere to hide
in this city of concrete. As if on cue,

she fluffs up her hair and pouts her lips.
Trucks slow, and a thunderclap shivers

from the Hollywood Theatre. She kneels,
shining, in the wet cement

as pellets of rain shoot off of her skin,
lights on the marquee going round.

The Swimming Mothers

It's like being dropped into a fishtank—
plastic treasures fanning alongside a school
of little darlings. And the pedicures!
Technicolor fins with lipsticks
and headbands to match.
I've never been a strong swimmer.
My father was afraid to see me
floating on my back in a shallow pool.
Today my eldest son makes his first dive,
stroking and gliding in water
over ten feet deep. But
the Swimming Mothers
ruin it for me. They talk
through gills, side-mouthed,
words so bloated one could
drown in the dialogue.
Sitting opposite, I see
their bodies merge like some
malformed sea animal,
wearing the species imprint
of Gucci and Versace. Up close
the women are lovely, impassive.
Faint flaws lie in the hands of their surgeons
stitched with hush money. Grouped together
they become this competing creature,
humpbacking on the waves
of husband's salaries
and children's test scores.
I imagine them later in kitchens
sneaking cigarettes,
or opening thighs for sex
with obligatory yawns,
their kind exhausted
by duty and boredom,
by the books unread
and resentments swallowed,
breeding toward extinction.

Shrink-Wrapped

How did she arrive
at such a little life?
Where she spends several days
scheduling her book return to the library.

Where the crumbs on her kitchen counter
worry her for hours.
Where she won't wipe them up for fear
of losing something to do.

Where she creeps through every room
adjusting pictures a few millimetres,
until they're all slightly crooked.

Where she tears out
page after page in her journal,
because there is no one to see,
nothing to write.

Where the gas-meter man
will knock repeatedly for days,
and she pretends not to hear.

Where the walls begin to bend
during certain rainy weeks,
making it impossible to breathe.

Where she eats the same meal
for three weeks running.
Where she never enters a bank.
Where she never learns to drive.

Where she never talks, not even to herself.

Where she obsesses over
airlock freezer bags,
their plastic sweetness,
breathless perfection.

Or sheets of Saran Wrap,
the snapped invisibility;
how wonderful they feel
clinging wordless to her skin.

Until she's finally sealed
into this silent world,
spotless and magical,
shrinking forever
within her little life.

Karma

My past lives are waiting
on hangers to be reborn:

Victorian mourning clothes
with antique buttons,

rawhide vests pasted
with steel magnolias.

When I open the closet
they huddle together,

trying to block me
from reading their auras.

I hear whispers as I fly past
the rayon and linen,

silk and denim. I meet fashion rejects
dancing with see-through night-gowns:

the modest, tattooed, pierced and cloned.
I'm stunned by this clash of colours,

by the whore-ish banging
of velvet against polyester.

And the shoes, please, can we talk?
Leathery veilings of erotic toe cleavage.

Why are these rags crushed
and crushing my closet?

There are so many lessons
they haven't learned yet.

In their next incarnation, I'm sure
they'll wake deified in a resale bin,

blessed by the cone-shaped Wonder Bra
Madonna saw the light in.

Him

I'm far enough away to make this possible:
rearrange opinions of him like furniture.
Compare the violet lining around his eyes
to the bedcover in that motel—

the one where he put the quarter in
to make the bed shake. He had
excuses each time for meeting me
except real ones: a drink, quick fuck.

Hoping I wouldn't notice how much
he talked about his mother's hair
once being my colour—
red as a whore's dress;
as sky exhaling over us, lung tissue.

In February looking up and out
the window of a '60 Chevy
and wondering when the glow
was going to start. Remembering's
easy as knocking over a table or chair.

Anytime I stick my nose in an old car
I hear our words mingling like down
falling out of a pillow. "Did you see it,
that red spark over the hill?"

The comet Kohoutek, practically invisible,
was his last excuse for driving to
an unfinished highway in the middle
of a Texas prairie. For a sight

that was supposed to rivet me
to another galaxy. That's when
the glow started and I didn't have to
fumble with the divider in the front seat
or comb my hair or even put the quarter in.

Goodbye

Slurp of moon
cupped over neighbouring houses,
brimming with gold liquid
ready to spill, ready to take me
someplace I need to go
on a whim.

I was pacing the floors
worrying over illusions too great to mention,
and too mind-bending for confession
one week later.

I want it back. That moon.
When I got up the next night
I spied my satiny pillow friend
on *Late Night with Conan O'Brien.*

Always liked that guy
after seeing him brave the moors—
Stonehenge and obscure, abandoned castles,
proving his ancestry to insomniac Americans
and other unsung barbarians.

He had my baby-stitched moon
tacked onto music stands and drumsets.
It hovered over his head
while he interviewed starlets.

I need that moon this instant,
because it reminds me to breathe
when loved ones leave town—
as I live life in the Poet's Lane,
waiting for muse-like manna
to drop hot onto my page.

Haven't I read *Goodnight Moon*
a million times? Okay, a million and one.
And did that Pillsbury crescent
turning unnaturally golden
in its time-warped pan,
ever hope for more? Maybe.

Don't you dare think what you're thinking.

I won't say goodbye.
This fantasy is real,
and tells me I'm stricken
with anger and contentment.

I hear Conan and his crusty
doughboys greasing more viewers.
Their giggles join Heathcliff's whisky cry
over the moonswept heather,
a raging, magnificent storm.

Notes on the Poems

The older I get the more reluctant I am to explain why I think or do just about anything. Especially with poetry, it's better to have one's poems simply read, absorbed, experienced. But the work that eventually became *Your Last Day on Earth* went through so many transformations, some notes might prove illuminating.

The last four lines of "Brahms & Angelo's Garage" refer to the discovery of a tape found in the New York Philharmonic Archives of a live radio broadcast. The tape was remastered, complete with Leonard Bernstein's famous disclaimer that he didn't agree with Glenn Gould's chosen tempi for the Brahms D minor Concerto. In "Playing Mr. J.S. Naked" the line "Baroque version of Oscar Peterson" refers to the fact that *the old wig*, as Bach's sons called him, could improvise a seven-voice fugue with multiple key changes at the drop of a hat, a feat comparable to modern-day jazz artists. "Ripped Off" and "Miss _____" are different takes on my work as a piano examiner.

In reading "Towering Hibiscus" it may be helpful to know that the hibiscus bloom rarely lives for more than twenty-four hours and tends to send out single, not double or multiple blooms. And yet, one late summer day in my small garden its habits changed inexplicably. I wrote "Nightshine" long before I read the thoroughly researched biography of Emily Dickinson, *My Wars Are Laid Away in Books* by Alfred Habegger. When I did, I came across an intriguing description of her in 1876: "As they reached the eastern gate of the garden they espied Emily, all in white, among her flowers." The mention of Rodin at the end of "In the Garden" refers to Rodin's reluctance (or inability) to finish his masterpiece *The Gates of Hell*, over a twenty-year period. When it suited him he broke certain pieces off, moved them around, much like a writer plays with text. Finally, months after choosing the epigraph at the start of the section "Flowering," I learned that Georgian poet Edward Thomas was tragically killed serving England during World War I. "Lights Out" was written while he was waiting to go into battle, and is not only about one person's courageous last day on earth, but shows how well he spent it – writing poems.

Carla Hartsfield
Toronto, May 26, 2003.

Acknowledgements

Some of these poems have previously appeared in *Plus Zero, The Lazy Writer, Arc, The Fiddlehead, The Gaspereau Review,* and *New Texas 2002* (USA). "Queen Anne's Lace" and "In The Space That My Father Left" were published in the 2001 spring and fall issues of *Kalliope* (USA) along with the transcript of an interview later televised by PBS as "Writer To Writer." "At the Textile Museum" and "Anonymous" were commissioned in September, 2000, by the Textile Museum of Canada to celebrate their 25th anniversary. A few poems were self-published as a limited edition chapbook titled, *The Moon Pool* (New Notes, Inc., 1998).

Selections from *Your Last Day on Earth* were also published in the following anthologies: *Understatement* (Seraphim Editions, 1996), *The Edges Of Time* (Seraphim Editions, 1999), *What Have You Lost?* (Greenwillow Books, NY, 1999) *New Canadian Poetry* (Fitzhenry & Whiteside, 2000) and *New Century North American Poets* (River King Press, USA, 2002). "Black-Eyed Susans" is forthcoming in *Is This Forever Or What? Poems & Painting From Texas,* edited by Naomi Shihab-Nye (Greenwillow Books, NY, 2004).

Many thanks to my editor, Barry Dempster, for his belief in my work, sharp insights, intelligence and friendship. And to other fellow porch sitters, especially Laura Lush, for tireless ears and advice. Thanks also to John Garmon for years of encouraging correspondence during the making of this book. To Linda Cooper for allowing me to write in her beautiful healing space, Angel Shadows. To Marg MacIver and the nuns of St. Joseph for their spiritual guidance and peaceful retreats, which continue to renew my energy and vision.

Last but not least, heartfelt thanks to my husband Kenn and our sons Alex and John, for their love and understanding (and for never complaining when it's necessary to close my office door).

Carla Hartsfield

was born in Waxahachie, Texas, a farming community south of Dallas. She is a classically trained pianist, winning competitions and the National Piano Guild's Paderewski Medal before immigrating to Canada. Carla has published two previous poetry collections with Véhicule Press/Montreal—*The Invisible Moon* (1988), shortlisted for the Gerald Lampert prize, and *Fire Never Sleeps*, which was added to the Sylvia Plath archives at Smith College for its series of poems based on that poet's letters and journals. Carla has published widely in the U.S. and Canada and is also a singer/songwriter as well as a self-taught autoharp player. *River Called Night*, her first commercial CD, was released in 2000.